A
Is for Altar
B Is for Bible

Art and text by Judith Lang Main

**Catechesis of
the Good Shepherd
Publications**

A IS FOR ALTAR, B IS FOR BIBLE copyright © 2002 Archdiocese of Chicago: Liturgy Training Publications, 3949 South Racine Avenue, Chicago IL 60609; 1-800-933-1800, fax 1-800-933-7094, e-mail orders@ltp.org. All rights reserved. See our website at www.LTP.org.

This book was edited by Margaret M. Brennan. Audrey Novak Riley was the production editor. The design is by Anna Manhart, and the typesetting was done by Jim Mellody-Pizzato in Mrs Eaves. Printed in the United States of America.

Catechesis of the Good Shepherd Publications is an imprint of Liturgy Training Publications (LTP). Further information about its books, journals, and other products is available from LTP or from Catechesis of the Good Shepherd, 7655 East Main Street, Scottsdale, AZ 85251. Requests for information about other aspects of the Catechesis should be directed to this address.

Library of Congress Control Number: 2002114271

20 19 18 17 16   3 4 5 6 7

ISBN 978-1-56854-458-8

ABCD

This book is dedicated with love and gratitude

to

my husband, Rich,

my parents, Dot and Bill,

and my children, Nora, Paul and Martha

A Is for Altar, B Is for Bible is about significant and indispensable aspects of our Christian faith. As Christians we search for ways to share the mysteries of our faith with our children. Just as we teach our children the ABCs to help them learn to read and write, we seek ways to share fundamental beliefs, the ABCs of our faith, with them.

This small booklet offers an alphabet of our faith.

When we gather around the altar and when we read the Bible, we encounter symbols, objects, people and stories that tell us about God and God's life with us. *A Is for Altar, B Is for Bible* is intended more as an experience than an education. Young children are capable of experiences of all kinds, including the ability to glimpse the divine in the midst of the everyday.

The three- and four-year-olds of my acquaintance are experts at discovering God anywhere and everywhere.

I remember being a three-year-old.

At that time the essence of heaven for me was:
    a beautiful picture book,
    a lap in which to nestle,
    arms enfolded around me,
    a loving voice to read the words
    and best of all, the occasional whispered invitation
      to me to turn the page.

From this early experience comes my desire to share simple words and images of our faith. May you and your children enjoy many holy moments together.

Judith Lang Main

Aa Bb Cc

Gg Hh Ii Jj

Nn Oo Pp

Uu Vv Ww

Dd Ee Ff

Kk Ll Mm

Qq Rr Ss Tt

Xx Yy Zz

is for
altar

I will go to the altar of God,
to God my exceeding joy.

Psalm 43:4a

B

is for

Bible

Your word is a lamp to my feet
and a light to my path.

Psalm 119:105

C

is for

chalice

Then Jesus took a cup, and after giving thanks
he gave it to them.

Mark 14:23

D

is for
delight

When they saw that the star had stopped,
they were overwhelmed with joy.

Matthew 2:10

E

is for
Elizabeth

When Elizabeth heard Mary's greeting,
the child leaped in her womb.

Luke 1:41

is for

font

Create in me a clean heart, O God.

Psalm 51:10

is for

good shepherd

The good shepherd calls his own sheep by name
and leads them out.

John 10:3b

is for

hidden treasure

The kingdom of heaven is like treasure
hidden in a field.

Matthew 13:44

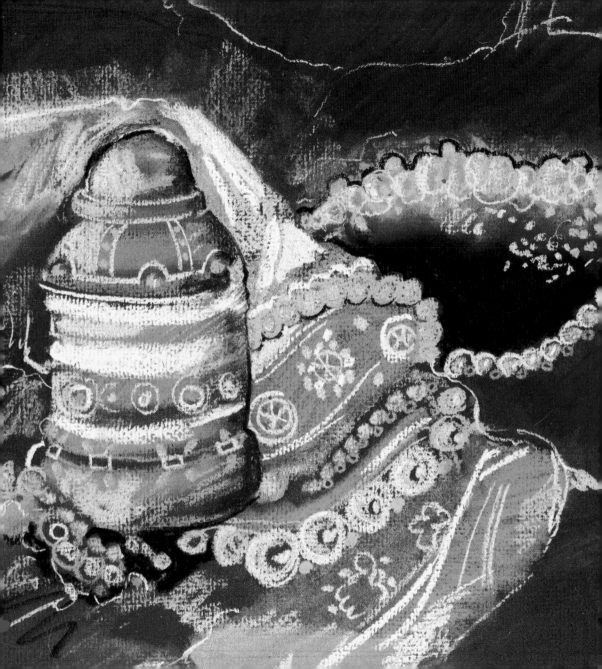

is for

Isaiah

The people who walked in darkness
have seen a great light.

Isaiah 9:2

J

is for Jerusalem

Jerusalem—built as a city:
Pray for the peace of Jerusalem.

Psalm 122:3a, 6a

K

is for

kingdom of God

The kingdom of heaven
is like a mustard seed.

Matthew 13:31

L

is for

light

I am the light of the world.

John 8:12

M

is for

Mary

Mary said, "Here am I, the servant of the Lord;
let it be with me according to your word."

Luke 1:38

is for

Nazareth

The angel Gabriel was sent by God
to a town in Galilee called Nazareth.

Luke 1:26

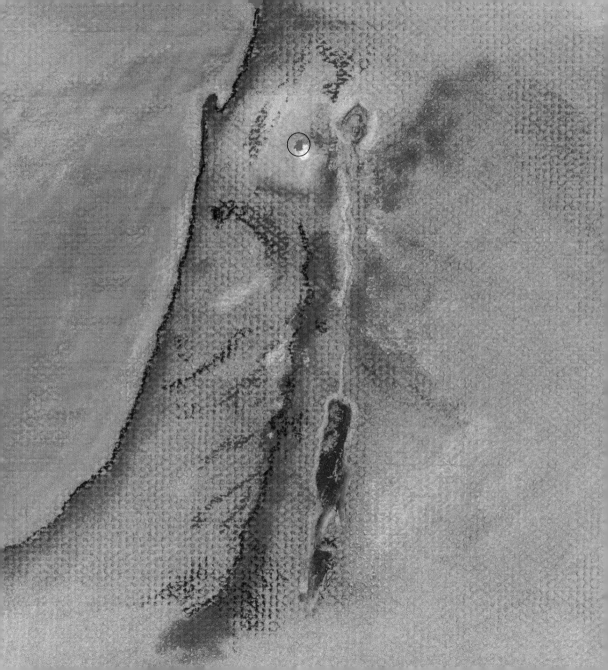

is for

oil

You anoint my head with oil.

Psalm 23:5b

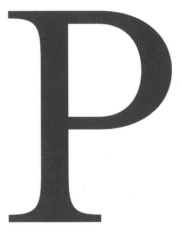

P

is for

pearl

The kingdom of heaven is like a merchant
in search of fine pearls.

Matthew 13:45

is for quiet

He leads me beside still waters;
he restores my soul.

Psalm 23:2b—3a

R

is for

resurrection

And very early on the first day of the week,
when the sun had risen,
they went to the tomb.

Mark 16:2

S

is for

Simeon

Now there was a man in Jerusalem
whose name was Simeon
. . . and the Holy Spirit rested on him.

Luke 2:25

T

is for

temple

We ponder your steadfast love,
O God, in the midst of your temple.

Psalm 48:9

U

is for

understanding

The spirit of the LORD shall rest on him,
the spirit of wisdom and understanding.

Isaiah 11:2

is for

vestment

Of the blue, purple, and crimson yarns
they made finely worked vestments,
for ministering in the holy place.

Exodus 39:1

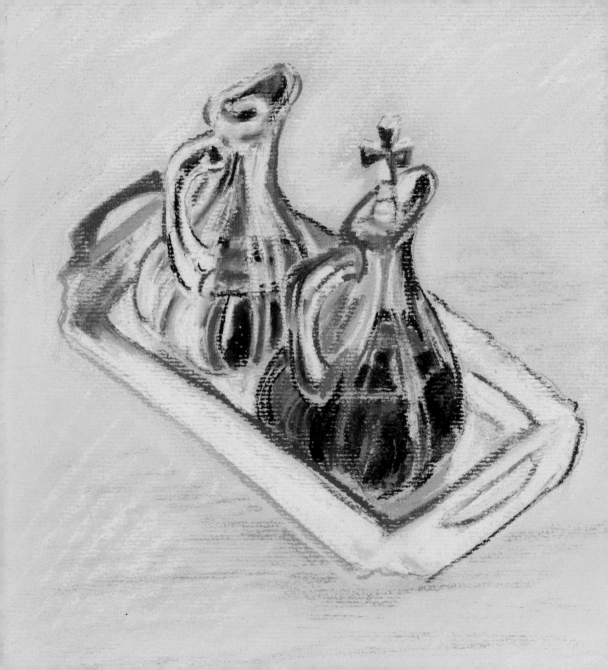

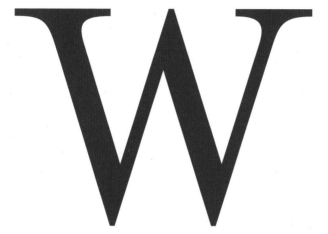

W

is for

water and wine

By the mystery of this water and wine
may we come to share in the divinity of Christ.

Roman rite, preparation of the gifts

X

is at the end of

crucifix

I lay down my life for the sheep.

John 10:15b

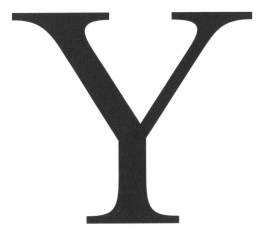

is for

yeast

The kingdom of heaven is like yeast that a woman took
and mixed in with three measures of flour
until all of it was leavened.

Matthew 13:33

Z

is for

ZZZZZZ

I lie down and sleep;
I wake again, for the LORD sustains me.

Psalm 3:5

A	altar	At Mass we gather around a table called the altar.
B	Bible	The Bible is a sacred book that tells us about God. It is the word of God.
C	chalice	The chalice is the cup that contains the wine at Mass.
D	delight	Delight means to be filled with joy, to enjoy completely.
E	Elizabeth	Elizabeth, Mary's cousin, is the mother of John the Baptist.
F	font	The font holds the water for baptism. It is usually made of stone.
G	good shepherd	Jesus is the good shepherd who knows and loves each sheep by name.
H	hidden treasure	Jesus told a story about a treasure hidden in a field.
I	Isaiah	Isaiah was a great prophet who foretold the birth of the Messiah.

J	Jerusalem	Jerusalem is the city in Israel where Jesus offered his life for all people.
K	kingdom of God	Jesus told many parables or stories about the kingdom of God.
L	light	Jesus is the light of the world. We are children of the light when we follow him.
M	Mary	Mary is the mother of Jesus. We pray, "Hail Mary, full of grace."
N	Nazareth	Nazareth is the small town where Mary and Joseph and Jesus lived and worked and prayed.
O	oil	Holy oils are blessed by the bishop and are used in the sacraments of baptism, confirmation, anointing of the sick and holy orders.
P	pearl	Jesus told a parable about a merchant searching for the one most beautiful pearl.
Q	quiet	When it is quiet we can be aware that God loves each of us.
R	resurrection	We celebrate Jesus' resurrection from the dead at Easter.

S	Simeon	Simeon was a holy man who recognized Jesus as God's son.
T	temple	The temple, a place for prayer and worship, was in Jerusalem.
U	understanding	At Pentecost we ask the Holy Spirit for the gift of understanding.
V	vestment	At Mass the priest wears a vestment. There are different colors of vestments for the different seasons.
W	water and wine	At Mass the priest pours a few drops of water into the wine. They mingle together.
X	crucifix	The crucifix is a sign of God's love for us.
Y	yeast	Leaven is another name for yeast. It makes bread rise.
Z	zzzzzz	Zzzzzz stands for sleep. Even when we sleep, God is giving us life and love.

The Catechesis of the Good Shepherd

The Catechesis of the Good Shepherd was begun in Rome over fifty years ago by Sofia Cavalletti and her Montessori collaborator, Gianna Gobbi. Today the Catechesis can be found in nineteen countries around the world.

This approach to religious formation offers an opportunity for adults and children to share their faith life together. They meet in a specially prepared room called the atrium, the ancient name of the place near the church where early Christians prepared to enter more fully into the community of faith.

In this atrium the children use simple, beautiful materials to meditate on the scriptures, the liturgy and the sacraments. Order, repetition and movement are some of the principles that allow the children to make both liturgical and scriptural components of our faith a part of their everyday life.

This alphabet book includes many of the themes of the Catechesis for young children, ages three to six. Infancy narratives, kingdom parables, maps and place names, and articles from the Mass are each given a moment of focus.

Quietly pondering these words and images can nurture the child's knowledge and love of God. It is the meeting of the mystery of God and the mystery of the child that gives the Catechesis of the Good Shepherd its life.

More information about the Catechesis can be found on the Internet at www.cgsusa.org.

A Note from the Artist

I enjoy working with pastels because the pigment and the paper are right there waiting to connect— no paintbrush in between.

In much the same way, God and the children are waiting to connect. My work over the years in the Catechesis of the Good Shepherd has filled me with wonder and awe. I have used lots of pastels attempting to put this wonder down on paper.

Margaret Brennan and Anna Manhart at LTP have given generously of their time and talent.

Working to unite both hearts and hands, Sofia Cavalletti and Gianna Gobbi have inspired hundreds of catechists to roll up their sleeves and become workers in God's kingdom. I am very grateful to be a part of that wonderful community.

I give special thanks to the Saint Catherine atrium children for helping me with the images for many of the letters—to Oliver for the font, to Fiona for Jerusalem, and also to John in Memphis.

I was inspired by the Magadan experience of the Madonna House community and am grateful to them for images of children at work and prayer.

Infancy narrative figures from many atriums as well as our own have given me ideas for arrangements and set-ups. It is truly the work of many hands.

AVERY PHOTOGRAPHY, INC.

And finally, the partnership with Rich Main in atrium material making as well as in life has given me more than words or pictures in pastels could ever say.

About the Artist

Judith Lang Main is a catechist and religious education coordinator at Saint Catherine Parish in Milwaukee, Wisconsin. She has served on the board of the National Association of the Catechesis of the Good Shepherd and is a formation leader and trainer in the Catechesis.